Goldilocks and the Three Bears

Moira Butterfield

Heinemann Library
Des Plaines, Illinois

© 1998 Reed Educational & Professional Publishing
Published by Heinemann Library,
an imprint of Reed Educational & Professional Publishing,
1350 East Touhy Avenue, Suite 240 West
Des Plaines, IL 60018

Editor: Alyson Jones
Designer: Joanna Hinton-Malivoire
Illustrator: Barbara Vagnozzi
Printed and bound in Italy

02 01 00 99 98
10 9 8 7 6 5 4 3 2 1

Library of Congress Cataloging-in-Publication Data

Butterfield, Moira, 1961-
    Goldilocks and the three bears / Moira Butterfield.
        p.   cm. — (Puppet play)
    Summary: Provides instructions for making stick puppets, props,
and a theater along with a simple, easy-to-follow play script based
on the well-loved folktale.
    ISBN 1-57572-720-X (library binding)
    1. Puppet plays, American—Juvenile literature. 2. Puppet
theater—Juvenile literature. [1. Fairy tales—Drama. 2. Puppet
plays. 3. Puppet theater.] I. Goldilocks and the three bears.
English. II. Title. III. Series: Butterfield, Moira, 1961-
Puppet play.
PN1980.B9 1998
791.5'38—dc21   97-42685
                                                              CIP
                                                               AC

Always be careful when using scissors and glue to make the puppets and
props for your play. Make sure there is an adult to help you. Please use
non-toxic paints. You can find paint stirring sticks at a hardware store.

CONTENTS

 Reading the Play 4

 Making Puppets 6

 Making Props 8

 Making a Theater 9

 The Play 10

INTRODUCTION TO GOLDILOCKS

Goldilocks is a naughty, nosy girl who creeps into the Three Bears' house while they are away. Now you can make some finger puppets to act out their story and discover what happens to Goldilocks.

READING THE PLAY

Four puppet characters appear in this play:

Goldilocks
A naughty, nosy little girl

The Three Bears
Papa, Mama, and Baby Bear

Sometimes the **Puppeteer** speaks. That's the person who works the puppets.

Do this part in an ordinary voice.

If you want to perform this story as a puppet show there are some tips for you on pages 6-9.

If you prefer, ignore the stage directions and read the play with a friend. Divide the parts between you.

The play is made up of lines. Next to each line there is a name so you know who should be speaking.

Goldilocks

> I'm so naughty. I've crept into the Bears' house while they are away. I like being nosy.

Sometimes there are stage directions. They are suggestions for things you can make puppets do at a performance.

Move Goldilocks around the stage as if she's being nosy.

MAKING PUPPETS

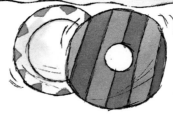

1. Cut along the side of an empty paper towel roll. Roll and tape the tube around your index and middle fingers.

4. Using the dinner plate as a template, cut the fabric into a circle. Cut a smaller circle in the center.

2. Cut the sock in two as shown. Stuff the toe end with newspaper.

5. Secure the circle of fabric around the puppet's neck with an elastic band.

3. Put the stuffed sock over the cardboard tube and secure it with an elastic band. Make it into a head shape.

To work the puppet, put your first two fingers into the neck tube. Wiggle the puppet so it appears to be talking.

THREE BEARS DECORATION

Make three bear puppets the same way as Goldilocks. Use felt for their hair and scrap material to decorate their clothes.

Cut slits through the fabric for your thumb and third finger. Poke them through to give your puppet arms.

GOLDILOCKS DECORATION

Glue on yellow felt to make long hair. Decorate the dress with scrap material. Glue on cardboard pieces for her face.

MAKING PROPS

* Cardboard
* Paint stirring sticks
* Pencil and scissors
* Glue and scotch tape
* Cardboard, fabric, or paints to decorate props

PORRIDGE BOWLS

Copy this shape onto cardboard and cut it out. Paint each bowl differently and tape a stick firmly to the middle of the back.

BEAR CHAIRS

Cut out three armchair shapes. The one shown on the right is Mama Bear's chair. Papa Bear's chair should be slightly bigger, and Baby Bear's chair a little smaller.

Decorate each chair differently. Cut a small hole in the seat of Baby Bear's chair to show it is broken. Then tape a stick to the back of each chair.

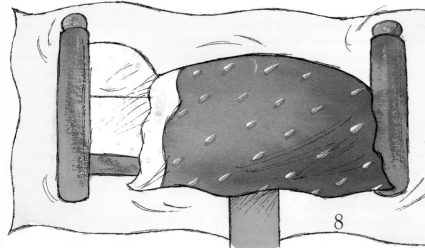

BEAR BEDS

Cut out three bed shapes. Decorate each of them differently and tape a stick to the back of each one.

8

MAKING A THEATER

 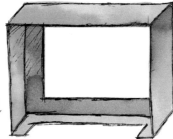

1. Cut the two large boxes as shown. Tape back any strips that fall off and tape all the joints to make they are secure.

WHAT YOU NEED

* **Two large-sized cereal boxes**
* **Two medium-sized cereal boxes**
* **Colored paper or paints**
* **Glue and tape**
* **Scissors**

2. Glue the two together as shown and add some tape to make the joint really strong. Glue and tape a medium-sized box on each side to help your theater stand up.

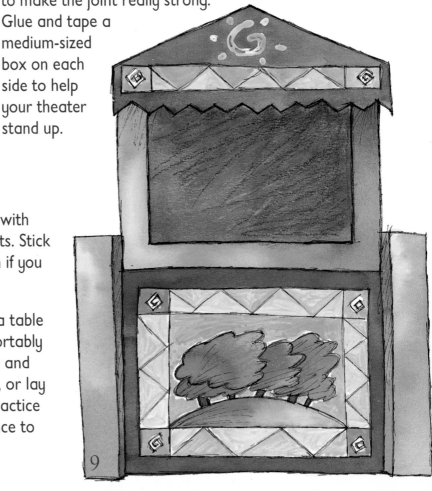

3. Decorate the theater with colored paper or paints. Stick extra cardboard shapes on if you like, such as a pointed top.

4. Stand the theater on a table so you can hide comfortably behind it with your puppets and book. Prop the book inside, or lay it flat on the table. Then practice before you invite an audience to watch your play.

GOLDILOCKS AND THE THREE BEARS

Start by putting your head up and talking to the audience.

Puppeteer

Hello everyone. The star of my play has long yellow hair and she's very naughty. Can you guess who she is?

Put your head down and put up Goldilocks, then the three Bears. Say, "hello" each time in a different voice.

Goldilocks

Here I am. My name is Goldilocks.

Papa, Mama, and Baby Bear

Hello.

Take down all the Bears. Put up Mama Bear and the porridge bowls prop.

Mama Bear

Here we are, Bears. Yummy hot porridge for breakfast.

Wiggle Mama Bear as she eats the porridge. Make some eating noises.

Mama Bear

Ouch, that burned my tongue! It's far too hot to eat now. Let's go out for a walk and let it cool down.

Take Mama Bear off but keep the porridge bowl prop on.

Hold up Goldilocks.

Goldilocks

> I'm so naughty. I've crept into the Bears' house while they are away. I like being nosy.

Move Goldilocks around the stage, as if she's being nosy.

Goldilocks

> Hmm, let's have a look around.

Stand Goldilocks behind each porridge bowl, one by one. Start with the biggest.

Goldilocks

Yum, yum. Three bowls of porridge. I think I'll try them all.

Make eating noises.

Goldilocks

Yuck. This big bowl is too salty.
Yuck. This middle-sized bowl is too sweet.

Mmmm. This little bowl is just right.

Goldilocks

Make some more eating noises.

What a shame. It's all gone.

Goldilocks

Take the porridge bowl prop away and hold up Papa Bear's chair.

14

Move Goldilocks in front of the chair.

I think I'll sit and rest for awhile....I don't like this big chair. It's not comfortable at all.

Goldilocks

Change chairs and hold up Goldilocks in front of Mama Bear's chair.

This middle-sized chair is too lumpy. It makes me ache!

Goldilocks

Now hold up Baby Bear's chair with Goldilocks in front so the hole is hidden.

Goldilocks

> This little chair is just right....
> Oooh, I've broken it!

Move Goldilocks to show the hole.

Goldilocks

> Oh well, I think I'll go and be nosy upstairs.

Take away the chair and put the beds up one at a time. Hold Goldilocks up in front of each one. Start with Papa Bear's bed.

I think I'll try the beds. This big one feels too hard for bouncing.

Goldilocks

Hold up Goldilocks in front of Mama Bear's bed.

Mmm...This middle-sized one feels too soft.

Goldilocks

Hold up Baby Bear's bed.

This little bed is comfy. I think I'll take a nap.

Goldilocks

Make yawning noises. Then take Goldilocks and the bed down out of sight.

18

Put up the porridge bowl prop. Then hold up one Bear at a time behind each bowl. Make sure you hold each Bear up behind the right sized bowl.

Papa Bear

This porridge should be cool enough now. Hey, someone's been eating my porridge.

Mama Bear

Someone's been eating my porridge.

Baby Bear

Someone's been eating my porridge and now it's all gone!

Take down the bears and the bowls. Put up the chairs one by one. Hold up one bear at a time behind each chair.

Papa Bear

Someone's been sitting in my chair.

Mama Bear

Someone's been sitting in my chair.

Baby Bear

Someone's been sitting in my chair and they've broken it!

Take down Baby Bear and the chair. Hold up the beds one at a time. Hold up each bear behind them.

Papa Bear

Someone's been sleeping in my bed.

Mama Bear

Someone's been sleeping in my bed.

Hold up Goldilocks so the back of your hand faces the audience. Use your other fingers and thumb to hold the little bed behind her. Hold Baby Bear in the other hand.

Baby Bear

Someone's been sleeping in my bed, and here she is! Come here quickly!

Take Baby Bear off so you have one hand free.

Goldilocks

Oooh! Help!

Use your free hand to hold Goldilocks. Make her jump up and down.

Goldilocks

The bears are back!
They'll eat me!
Let me out!

Move Goldilocks off the side of the stage.

Stick your head up together with Goldilocks.

Puppeteer

The bears did not eat Goldilocks and she told them she was sorry.

Goldilocks

I'm sorry!

Put Goldilocks down and pick up Papa Bear to shake at the audience.

Puppeteer

I hope you are never naughty or nosy. If you are, an angry Bear might pay YOU a visit!

Papa Bear

Grrr!

THE END